Crucible

Library of Congress Cataloging-in-Publication Data

Bosch, Daniel.
    Crucible / Daniel Bosch.
        p. cm.
    ISBN 1-59051-020-8 (hardcover)
    1. Title.

PS3602.O83 C78 2002
811'.6—dc21

                                                    2001059427

Crucible

Daniel Bosch

HANDSEL BOOKS
an imprint of
Other Press • New York

This book is for Michaela, part of whose crucible I am.

I wish to express my thanks to the many poets who have been so generous in offering critical responses to the poems in this volume.

Grateful acknowledgment is made to the editors of the following magazines in which many of the poems in *Crucible* have appeared:

Harvard Review "The Crucible"
Gulf Coast "Homage to Christopher Smart," "The New Life," Passion Fruit (11 poems)
Del Sol Review "Johnson to Berkeley on Telegraph" (as "Bishop Berkeley on Telegraph")
Salamander "In Memory of Derek Walcott"(as "Elegy"), "Far From Earth"
Partisan Review "Home Thoughts from Aboard Continental Flight 94"
The New Republic "Robert Bly Quelling Riots in Miami"
Agni "Dear Mom," "Erato in Hollywood"
Bostonia "Invitation to Ms. Jorie Graham," "Tree of Knowledge"
New CollAge Magazine "Contents of a Jar"
Boston Review "'Philadelphia,' Starring Tom Hanks,"
    "'Big,' Starring Tom Hanks,"
    "'Apollo 13,' Starring Tom Hanks,"
    "'Forrest Gump,' Starring Tom Hanks"
The Literary Review "BAM!"
Sarasota Review of Poetry Passion Fruit (14 poems)

Contents

Passion Fruit

Homages & Elegies

The Crucible

After virtue, under the eye of the clock,
Patterns of culture in our time, our bodies,
Ourselves, let us now praise famous men,
Invisible cities, pride and prejudice.

After Babel, to the land of the cattails,
Tender is the night of grammatology,
The well-wrought urn, silence in the snowy fields,
Paradise lost from here to eternity.

Other criteria hopscotch on liberty,
On deconstruction, on dreams.
The separate notebooks cry, "the beloved country."
Mimesis travels with Charley, islands in the stream

Marry me. Far from the madding crowd, the possessed
Bang the drum slowly against interpretation,
Pale fire, men and women, labyrinths, the best
Short stories of 1988, civilization

And its discontents. Languages of art,
I know why the caged bird sings:
To have and have not a part of speech,
Of time and the river, the order of things.

Pride's Round

Proud as I am, Michaela, proud as I am
Of my eyes' blue in yours, your hand in mine,
I gather with your bones dry sticks of blame,
And catch in tears the scent of gasoline:
Though being true to you is my desire
In being true, I place sticks on your pyre.

In being true, I place sticks on your pyre,
Building a nest our likeness will ignite.
You match my sticks, and my yarns' ligatures
Fasten us bone to bone and like to like.
Though I grow warm to see myself return
In you, I dread how brightly I must burn.

In you I dread how brightly I must burn,
How I'll survive as fuel for your cremation,
How you will curse my bones because you learned
To strike hot flame from my flint inspiration.
So tears from your blue eyes do whet my shame,
Proud as I am, Michaela, proud as I am.

Homage to Christopher Smart

Pity, the lump in your own throat.
Self-pious Pity; Pity the wishbone.
Pity, the self-employed esthetician
Contracted for us by the government.
Pity, the shingle. Pity, the physician.
Pity, sipped from an inverted paper cone.

Self-Pity, brought up on riot charges,
Standing before His Honor in an orange jumpsuit.
Pity fining Self-Pity for contempt of court.
Self-Pity, its justified margins,
Its inverted exclamation points, its square roots.
Self-Pity, selling itself short.

Pity pinned in among rejected cornerstones.
Self-Pity, absent without leave,
Waiting in the aisle for the collection plate.
Pity rolling up Self-Pity's sleeves
For lethal injection; Pity come too late,
Huffing and sweating, grown fat on bread alone.

Pity, the words that never hurt you.
Self-Pity, asking Pity about the bells.
Pity in another life, admiring
Self-Pity's vacation home, its 360° view,
Totally unobstructed. Isn't it inspiring?
Pity, the answer. Pity, the one who tells.

The New Life

after Emily Dickinson

Musicians wrestle Everywhere.
It pins their shoulders to the ground.
It does a careful damage to their instruments
Called "wear and tear."
Musicians passing at the edge of town
Discuss their battered stands, their ligaments.

This way they avoid our divorce.
Playing tight duets,
Dusting off mustard yellow singlets
And monochromatic scales
Keeps them from saying we failed.
Musicians are good sports,

Love is a half-nelson and these half-notes
Choking me up come out of nowhere.
I want you on your back, and back.
I want to count to three and slap
My hand hard on a map to everywhere
Musicians go.

The words we said at the edge of towns
Were rounds. Everywhere we sang
Is marked by a pin and a melody.
The air is full of the scores of cities
Where music told me everything
But how to hold you close, or down.

Johnson to Berkeley on Telegraph

What do I know? Answers are subtle.
Check out that ass. I'm sure that butt'll
Tell all: the secrets Spandex™ keeps, expanded,
Suggest we were born under-handed.
Fistful disclosure, dark, stark abundance,
Reality, unbound, might seem redundance
Were it not so that perfect breasts have seams.
Enlarged? Reduced? It's all the stuff of dreams.

We wake. If Darwin's right, then reproduction's
Reason why: We do. We die. Liposuction?
Siliconic rhinoplasty? Tummy tuck?
And what of history? Should we not fuck
With the past? Why *not* become a virgin?
The ten deft digits of a surgeon
Can stop the dyke as sure as rhymin'
Knits a well-made stanza's hymen.

When hard, it's hard to be objective:
"Is your affinity elective,
Or are you just glad to see me?" Did HMOs
Provide these luscious curves life throws
My way? When is a hottie not a hottie?
I mean, is anybody anti-body?
What do I care? Rock bottoms are rock bottom.
Check that one out. What I know's I can spot 'em.

Falsetto

Esterina, your twenty years threaten you
like a grey-rose cloud
that little by little draws closed.
Yet this tightening doesn't frighten:
We see a girl who swims
under smoke the violent wind
rends, and gathers, and rends.
When the ashen swell expels you,
redder than ever, sun-fevered,
the arc of your back's a story
and your face is Diana's kissed
by her bow-string.
Your twenty falls climb
the rungs of past springs,
hugging you;
the ringing in your ears
presages the Elysian spheres'.
Let no one break the clay pots'
cracked silence! What you should hear
is an ineffable concert
of tinkling bells.

No doubt tomorrow doesn't scare you.
Graceful, taut on a wet rock,
glittering with salt, you burn
your limbs with sun.
Lizards are so fixed
on their bleak pedestals;
youth lies in wait for you
with his boy's noose, a loop of grass.
Water's power tempers you;
in water is recovery, in water, your renewal:
We think of you as seaweed, as a pebble,
a sea-made sea-maid
brine purifies
and returns to the shore unscathed.

And how right you are! The present
smiles—don't disturb it with worries.
Be gay—you have a date with the future
and a shrug of your shoulders
rocks strongholds, knocks over
the dark towers tomorrows build.
You stand up and step to the slender
gangplank below which Gorgons screech:
Your profile is etched
in silhouette against pearl.
You hesitate: The plank's edge trembles,
but then you laugh, a collapse
so complete it seems the wind has plucked you
or some divine friend taken you by the hand.

We are the race of watchers
who must remain on land.

Ice and Fire

The human who invented fire
Lay down upon a bed of ice,
Exhausted. It was her desire
To get the hell away from fire.
(She wouldn't need to test it twice.)
Then in blue sleep she dreamt up hate—
Deep glacial cuts, brute polar ice—
The motivation of the great.
Cool, she thought. Two suffice.

Nocturnal Transmission with Imagery as Attachment

(after Larkin)

I keep sending: I can't believe
    You really didn't love me,
But I don't believe it.
    I *do* believe. I was alone
In love. And now, alone, I grieve it.

Even my return key is depressed.
    I miss you. But I miss my doubt
More fiercely: Doubt made love possible.
    Doubtless I loved you, but, conversely,
I cannot doubt my love was misaddressed.

The system's mailer-daemon can admit
    It's ignorant, so who am I not to?
I don't know you. I never did,
    Or when I did, I didn't want to.
The Internet just sped up all this shit.

My programming makes it so damn
    Easy: it's as if it knows
I'll keep forming these attachments,
    That I'll point and I'll click and I'll
Virtually believe, especially at 3 a.m.

It's a kind of faith, a way of slowing down
    The accelerated pace of modern
Love—the dubious consumer consumed
    By keystrokes like "shift" and "control"
And the dim afterglow which love presumes.

In Memory of Derek Walcott

I

Cover Her Face.

If I take my grief to the beach
And scan my blurred reflection

As I slip it into a yellow Walkman—
If I hear only arias,

Only your words' permanent surf—
If I navigate the rectilinear

Terrycloth islands of Revere,
Ignore the cold water, the sorry-ass

Pilgrimage of pale, bony
Shadows, the nylon umbrellas'

Eerie, radial spectra,
The glint of my phony

Ray Bans—if I drag my empty leash
Past these bodies made of milk and honey

While gulls squabble over reddening girls,
Over turf, over nothing, but under every plane

That screams into Logan, its tail swaying
Left-right-left, like a runway model's—

It may be possible
To think that the shaded easel up ahead

Is your A-frame shelter here,
That it holds a final painting, a watercolor,

That the *Pitons* won't find their shallow
Images, sharp memories, too hard to swallow,

And that you, who have tuned out
Boom boxes and radios,

Will see me mouthing *adios.*

II

Mine Eyes Dazzle.

I spoke with Helen. We forgot the time.
The face that launched your thousand pages wore
A caul of wrinkles beautiful as rhyme.

Jim Crow's feet laced her eyes, and when she told
Of her long captive voyage in the hold
Of your imagination, we forgot the time.

We spoke of other men, the pain of snow,
The greenest islands glinting in your eye.
Her caul of wrinkles testified. Your rhyme

Rang in her voice, and so did her disdain
For those who seem to feel another's pain.
(One's own page should suffice.) Then Helen asked

If I adhered to your career advice:
"Be professional: Live off your wife.
This is a calling." Wrinkled, beautiful,

She smiled to think how foolish you had been
Ever to let her speak with other men.
I spoke with Helen. I will not forget
Her wrinkled face, her beauty like a net.

III

She Died Young.

When his brakelights embarrass St. Mary's street,
My cabbie kills the radio, turns up the heat,
And Charon or cherub, idling in the glare,
Waits for his fare.

Pastoral cold. I read between the blinds,
But infer no welcome: that was in my mind.
My eggshell trochees toward the cab aren't planned,
And yet they scan.

I speak to the mirror: "Take me to Logan."
The reflection grunts assent. He hasn't spoken,
Yet I have heard his accent, and knowing my islands,
Read his silence.

No man is insulated. From the tick of the meter,
From winter's dry grasp, from the gasp of the heater
Or the way a backseat horizontalizes,
Cuts down to size.

Apostrophes of steam mark cold contractions.
Boston's concrete begs for spare abstractions.
At five a.m., its stoplights mimic thinking
With bright blinking.

A full stop on Commonwealth. Pushing a cart, your
Narrow, shapka'd figure makes its departure
From the median—taking its time,
Like grief or rhyme,
Making little scarves with each exhaled breath
That do not warm him. He looks scared to death,
An exile who knows his hemisphere's
Too big. Up here,

An island is a platform where you pause
To look both ways before you safely cross,
Where you realize you've caused the world to wait—
To hesitate—

Where though you know you haven't got the power
To stretch those seconds into minutes, your
Ambition takes a step into the street
To find its beat.

Home Thoughts from Aboard Continental Flight 94

In memory of Joseph Brodsky

1

Horizontal Babel,
Your high-pitched hex
Hums in the grunting thrust
Of this plane leaving LAX.

Over the palm-lined, blue Pacific
Cruise ships proud as banks
Wink as I look down
On the land of the swank.

Oh, to be over America!
Where flight attendants' prose
Lulls the savage child
In each of thirty rows,

And I scan, in trimeter,
Dying for a hit,
The outlines of ghost cigarettes
They leave so brightly lit.

2

Mesas tabled when
Seas last litigated
Silently testify
On behalf of Time Incorporated.

The canyon's grand scansion
Is so irregular
The river must not know
The future of free verse—

Yet still its silt slowly
Reveals the past,
And layer by layer
Measures what lasts.

3

A checkerboard of farms
Gives way to greeny disks
Less perfect for bright barns'
Sudden radar blips

And skinny tangent highways
That bisect golden sheaves
Count the country's blessings
In lucky cloverleaves.

4

On midwest Sunday nights
The bare, bold parking lots
Of empty shopping malls
Wear only leopard spots.

So it seems the tiger
Has changed its stripes—
Or commerce here prefers
To choose its own disguise.

5

Manhattan gridlock's
Red and white glazes
Straighten incisors
Like a set of braces.

A smile I recognize—
Black bottom teeth, caries
Backlit by cavities
Full of actuaries—

But our nose wheel's skid
On Newark's hard tarmac
Brings me down again
With the Trade-Centered Karnak

That sparkles and shimmers
Like a wet, half-full cup
Of words I should know
But still have to look up.

Robert Bly Quelling Riots in Miami

You there! Did you know I wrote
a poem the day you were born? And every single day
I rise and measure myself against stones outside
that have millions of notches in them.
Stones like the one in your hand!

Once I had hair that made my body appear much larger.
Once I held a stone as you do now, and drove
a '65 Biscayne, bay-blue, beautiful
as prose. I have imagined myself
every bit as black as you, weeping
tears in the shapes of corn
that every man weeps whose skin has absorbed
the glare of floodlights, even in a barn.

Put down that stone! Or I will
refuse to write any longer. The stones of the earth,
like its children, should not be raised
as fists, but should settle, as I long to,
in my woman's lap, where ringless fingers
like young trees draw on my scalp
the world as it is.

Dear Mom

Lately poets have begun to think
Of language as a "subject," not a means
Used to achieve a goal they had in mind,
But the most important thing to write about,
Ur-topic and subtext, wizard behind
The pentametric curtain. It's enough,

Now, to promise poetry, enough
To cause a reader to think that they think
They've left the old life behind—
And the poems that went with it. No one means
Readers to care what a poem's "about"—
Rather they should be moved by how the mind

Shifts, symphonically, from word to word the mind
Will grasp as "tones." Mom, music is enough.
No self-respecting poet is about
To write a narrative poem they think
Is only narrative: "Story" means
Resolution, and resolution is behind

The times. Mom, our revolution is behind
Intelligent ambiguity. Never mind
How certain we are that our doubt means
More than your certitude; it's enough—
It would be enough—if you could think
Like me, for just a moment, think about

How all poems refer to themselves, about
Abstract diction, about what Ashbery means
When he claims not to know what to think.
I don't know how to confront a closed mind.
I keep thinking Keats but I don't have enough
"Negative Capability," whatever that means.

Why, Mom, does a poem have to be a means
To an end? Is it because your life's about
Over? Because your poems weren't enough?
I wish you could put all that behind
You. I wish you could make up your mind
Not to be bothered by what your kids think.

A poem means things never put behind it.
This poem is about a changing mind.
I know what you're thinking, and it's not enough.

Invitation to Ms. Jorie Graham

In Iowa City, in a jail of corn—taller than you are and more tasseled—
    live out your sentences.
In Iowa ice, in the dark of its aquifers,
    live out your sentences.
With the rising sun your warden
winking like meter on the floundering plains
and glazing the dullest park bench in Des Moines,
    live out your sentences.

Go ahead and ask about the klaxons and sirens. The church steeples
are breaking their ecumenical silences
having finally come to a point above Iowa.
Exit 37-A on I-80 is closed: an act of God,
a singularity, an opaque hailstone
big as a workshop but less likely to melt.
No one can pass it: Nobody still has plans.
The brittle corn shucks itself and smiles:
    Live out your sentences.

Stay for the bulbs you planted in velvety
peat moss that caught in your hair,
to gather your students' cocoons from still classrooms,
for your acolytes' writing, for the way they'd tug
at your velvet skirt if you tried to go—
    live out your sentences.

With Microsoft 6.0 at your feet,
with what you call thinking, draped in gypsy beads,
    live out your sentences.
Lies and silos fog the landscape; Iowa
rustles with Dasein on an ordinary evening,
    so live out your sentences.

Refusing verse technique, refusing to wait
for good lines while Romantic icons
back up like combines on state highways,
their idling engines' roar undreamt by taped philosophy
you rewind and rewind, savoring the fray
of Herr Professor's cut-off words, his fits and starts,
    live out your sentences.

Where convenience stores continuously welcome you,
where waiter is one letter away from writer,
where righteous white slats picket your departure
for every graduate seminar, then wait for your return
to your writing room and your desk,
    live out your sentences.
You can stand it there; you have the internet
and the arrangement of your fossil remains,
you have your students' parenthetical desires
for you to tell them who they are, so live,
    live out your sentences.

With critics' love, the love of only children,
opening crocuses and anthologies,
with spring fellowships blooming in your dooryard,
with bouquets of lilacs and corn silk,
     live out your sentences.

Wait out the sea's return to Iowa:
It is night and at this distance
your wavering spark is mistaken for Polaris
so please, in Iowa, in a cell of brittle stalks and leaves,
     live out your sentence.

Contents of a Jar

A crinkled paper makes a brilliant sound.
A mythology reflects its region. Here
In Oklahoma,

It is difficult to read. The page is dark.
The colorless light in which this wreckage lies
Falls, it appears, of its own weight to earth.

If from the earth we came, it was an earth
Tired of the old descriptions of the world,
The hand between the candle and the wall,

The poem and the mind in the act of finding
At night, by the fire,
The eye's plain version is a thing apart.

The poem must resist the intelligence.
Day is the children's friend.
Day creeps down. The moon is creeping up.

The skreak and skritter of evening gone
Proves that these opposite things partake of one,
And the night, and midnight, and after, where it is

Among twenty snowy mountains.
One must have a mind of winter
To speak quietly at such distance, to speak

The essential poem at the center of things,
This structure of ideas, these ghostly sequences
I figured you as nude between.

You speak. You say: Today's character is not
Clear water in a brilliant bowl,
Gloomy grammarians in golden gowns.

The truth is that there comes a time
In spite of hawk and falcon, green toucan,
These locusts by day, these crickets by night

Pour the unhappiness out
On the threshold of heaven, the figures in the street,
And this great esplanade of corn, miles wide,

Cries out a literate despair.
Another sunlight might make another world.
After the final no there comes a yes.

That strange flower, the sun,
Sister and mother and diviner love,
Finally, in the last year of her age,

Dissolved the distances of space and time
On her side, reclining on her elbow,
And sprawled around, no longer wild.

In English

You might begin by describing the river
you walk past every morning, the bridge
you cross, shoulder bags and hands full of books
you have read or will read and are sure
you understand. It could be anything, really.
You might say: "The bridge is a golden aisle..."

(We could object, of course, but only if
we acknowledge initially how much
we are ourselves responsible for what
we object to. A poem is an instrument.
We hold our own short hairs, and if you say,
we do so on a golden aisle.)

Our readers, who are uneven,
our lecturers, who are underpaid,
our professors, who pass us, waving, on
our way across this bridge, we all of us are
our own critique of each other. Repeat after me
Our creed:

I can diagram sentences with a straight face.
I can quote verbatim rules of grammar
I have learned in order to teach, not to say.
I can deny elementary resemblances
I have recognized in my heart from childhood.
I have learned never to say anything about

us—nodding at the sky or water flowing past
us is as close as I dare come. Between
us, only these pleasures: There is an
us, we can build no truth outside
us, and nothing, not even the river, can save
us. This much they know we know.

Erato in Hollywood

Plain purple t-shirt torn open,
Front-closing lace-front bra, unsnapped.
Red canvas espadrilles shoved in
Soft mud with blood almost black.

Belt loose of all but one belt loop.
Ratted hair trapped in wet bunches.
Hips small but arched like a roof
Raised by sharp stones at her haunches.

Bruises where a blue windbreaker's
Arms are pulled tight at her neck.
Upper arms broken in places
Exposed as she tried to deflect

More blows. Contusions on cheekbones.
Blood smear across lower spine.
Fingers of right hand grasp at stones
And four quarters form a vague line

Here to the road. Broken teeth, mud.
Underpants intact: No semen,
No stray pubic hair, no skin rubbed
Raw, but a saliva specimen

Dries on her still-extended
Left middle-finger as if
She wiped her lips as it ended
And flipped the camera off as she went stiff.

"Philadelphia," Starring Tom Hanks

after Mandelstam

The clots of burnt engine oil that sink into my vat
are so globular, so plastic, that as I pour I think:
"Nowhere else on Earth could such shit happen
that I would take an interest in." I watch them sink.

Next door they refuse to drink, as if the world didn't call for
cocktails and clowns. Don't go there. I'll tell you how it is:
days in piles, like unread sections of the newspaper.
They fight to ignore each other first, then pray in riots.

Until we suck down 7 UP, we keep to the black study.
The books show us their backsides before running away,
so we trace easy faces in the accumulated dust,
and wipe cool marble tables smooth as polished plains.

You say: "The raisins are dead. Delicious, but dead.
If they weren't wrinkled, we wouldn't know their ranks.
In 'Philadelphia' all hell broke loose, but here,
here there is only clean blood, and it is kept in banks.

Outside the plum-red room, all our noise comes unhemmed.
The attic, too, is bursting: How many vats of oil?
Don't forget what happened with the Frat: That guy we hated—
was it Kirk?—or Sammy?—Was he held responsible?

Black crude, black crude, burned and returned to the vat,
for how many miles did the tranny churn you
before those boys cracked their oil pan in our yard
and Jacqueline showed up, claiming she had nothing to do?"

"Big," Starring Tom Hanks

after Mandelstam

This is a Magic Kingdom. We must watch, not worry.
We must see like birds. We must pick up every pebble
fat Hansel drops. We must nest with our incredible
joysticks. (Without which there would be no story.)

Can you name the top five brands of tedium?
(Which is better than dying? They don't sell that here.)
We keep telling Hansel he has nothing to fear
from Mother Earth, a visual medium.

Outside Orlando, a liana noose
is common as mouse-ears. There's no news
on The Disney Channel. Is that good news?
You're hot as Hansel. Have an orange juice.

"Apollo 13," Starring Tom Hanks

after Mandelstam

Liftoff's gift is a Canaveral aurora,
a halo of orange thorns we tip back to see,
our hands raised to answer the shuttle's thunder...

We forget every perfect launch, every Saturn V
that wrote its sweet ant-track on a cake-blue sky.
(A Saturn V is like a good cigarette.)

It's not the smoke, then, not the eye-green sky,
but how long we stand and point. 'Houston, we have a problem.'
An embarrassing disaster: we glow like Granny Smiths.

At least we know the cause of our sudden deafness,
know why our astronauts stop looking back.
What's a fan's awe to a star's winking silence?

Which is only a refraction, Houston. Even tears refract.
Our tears are our haloes and first-stage boosters,
our Canaveral auroras and liftoff gifts.

"Forrest Gump," Starring Tom Hanks

after Mandelstam

1

This is the river that sees everything,
a mirror even after our hearts have raced
ahead, like stones, trailing bubbles from the trench,
while we, like Christ, step lightly to the other side.

The stars reflected in it haven't seen shit,
no matter what our horoscopes burn to say
or with what conviction. Let's call them "Pilate lights,"
and then, like Christ, step lightly to the other side.

It's hazy, hot, and humid. It's always been.
The ripe sun reaps a free lunch—"chef's surprise"—
and blindly Xs the river's face with stitches
like you'd get if you played hockey, or Christ.

Add to the list of humanity's successes—
such as the internet and tax free capital gains—
Professor Christ's alacrity with extensions.
This river never threatens when it rains.

(Anyway the arks are already built
and the pilots undergo yearly review
in simulators that simulate simultaneous
loss of power supply and crew.)

Gump, Forrest,
Congressional Medal of Honor winner,
this river's a grave. It knows your need for rest.
It knows you're a talker, not a listener.

2

Name a tectonic plate that doesn't practice
mutually assured destruction,
and then name one that really believes
it won't survive, lips hot with fiction,
pronouncing its new name, "Gaia,"
and teaching the stars how to spell it,
and using red lipstick to teach the stars.

3

Infinitesimal decimal points
queue up at the nursery window, one by one,
to view the absolute value—still moist,
spattered with sticky goose-egg shards—a son.

A plane of planes defines the plane—
Westmoreland's arms spread wide as a bunker.
Our sons make the kind of news we'll call intelligence
tomorrow, and forever, after the fighting.

Three points define us and our intelligence.
We lost at Dien Bien Phu. We won at My Lai.
We slept through Tet. When our planes grew light,
We ran from the orange glow, the fighting.

Which now seems like intelligence.
Which now seems as obvious and polite
as listening to the zip of a body bag
echo in defoliated night.

4

Kuwait was an Arabesque.
We ordered extra pixels and kept our distance.
Now Boeing builds us screen-sized nursery windows,
and we queue up for take-home Trans and Minhs.

And the best thing for the kids is to invest
in Boeing, in Raytheon, in United Technologies,
in crop circles, in the memory of those we saved
so much killing. Good Night Moon. Good Night Minh.

The natural consequences of air travel:
the duty-free purchases; the constant looking down,
like angels; the trenches filled with sand and pixels;
the earth in red lipstick; and burning refineries.

Up here we are close as family, as angels
crowding the heads of pins on strategic maps
or bending wheat stalks toward the centers of circles.
Our prayers are heard by the conservation of mass.

5

Think of pixels as light infantry,
as night's sweet chariots swinging low
over white teeth busy ants have flossed;
think of the clicks of your mouse as friendly fire,
your taut power cord as the string on a bow.
None of us are whole, but none of us
admit it. Instead we find jobs in light industry
and drink at home, watching T.V. as fine dust
gathers on Tiny Tim's remote control—
no one may use it now—that's what love costs!

6

In film there is the allegory of the bandage
doctors slowly unwind from a patient's skull:
Beneath the gauze, prepared to repel invasion,
the still-lit pilot lights, the windows to the soul.
In film no patient refuses the unwinding,
and the circle of doctors gasps at the miracles
of dilating and contracting decimals,
of irises the blues, greens, browns of Earth,
of sight's ovaries, its smooth *cojones* —for truly,
the skull has balls—it sees everything and says nothing.
Except "Here's mud in your eye, some silence you can sell."
Alas, empty sockets, you knew the patient well.

7

Like soldiers fanning out in patrols, bright sparks
leap from dark bivouacs with maps to the stars' homes
that are drawn on ash, and they faint when they see the stars
twinkling in Hollywood, or in poems.

The only people we really know are extras—
not even Oprah will step lightly to the other side—
but if the grave ahead outlives its reputation,
it's not because our astronauts haven't tried.

We pack our shuttles like phylacteries—
with bright sparks of prayer, with smoky poems
that read like intelligence—what with all the hurry
to leap from our dark bivouac to the stars' homes.

Yes, my conscience contracts, but it has a half-life
longer than Earth's embers, longer than chromosomes,
and if I'm called upon to give a toast,
I'll recite some optimistic poems.

By the hatch of the international space station
will they post a charm shaped like a T.V. console?

8

My heart, which I gladly drop into the river,
clocks against the others on the bottom:
"I was born in the year 'sixty-one,'"
"I was born in the year 'sixty-nine...'"
and I try to step lightly, try not to listen
to such spheres' music: On my numb tympanum
beats instead, with an internal shiver:
"I was born at seven-thirty a.m.
on August second in the year of sinus rhythm
nineteen sixty-two. I will live to hear
the lies of the third millennium."

Tree of Knowledge

If you know the name of the poem you would like to hear,
Press one, now.
To search the index for a poem or poet,
Press two, now.
For critical assessment of a poem,
Press three, now.
To speak with a poet, hold the line
Or press zero at any time.

The poem you have selected,
"Stopping by Woods on a Snowy Evening,"
Is currently in use. Please select another.
The poem you have selected,
"To Autumn," is currently in use.
Please select another.
The poem you have selected,
"Because I Could Not Stop for Death,"
Is no longer in service.
Please hold the line for critical assessment.

For definitions of kindness, press one, now.
To hear other reasons why Death stops,
Press two, now. If you feel as though
The top of your head has physically been taken off,
Press three, now. For other poems about Death,
Or for Death's current itinerary,
Hold the line and a poet will answer.

For "Thirteen Ways of Looking at a Blackbird,"
Press one, now.
If the mind of the tree and the mind of the bird are one,
Press two at any time.
To have a mind of winter,
Press three, now.
For ideas about the thing,
Press four, now.
For the thing itself, or to compose your own poem,
Please hold the line.

For the word, "heart," press one, now.
For the word, "tears," press two, now.
For the words, "Eye," "Cheek," "Lip," or "Brow,"
Search for Donne. When thou hast done,
Press three to return to the main menu.

The word "heart" is currently in use. Please select another.
The word "beating" is currently in use. Please select another.
The word "twittering" is no longer is service.
For help in choosing between two roads,
Please hold the line and a poet will answer.
To make it new, press pound.

For God's sake hold your tongue and let me love,
Press one, now.
If you can keep your head while those around you,
Press two, now.
To three posts driven upright in the ground,
Press three, now.
To reap a time to sow,
Please hold the line and a poet will ask you
If you know the name of the poem you would like to hear.

BAM!

'N I went BAM! wit my fist
In her gut 'n I said "Fuck
You, nigga, dat's for fuck'n

Wit my shit," 'n me 'n my
Girls, we done just bought some herb
'N shit, 'n that nigga she

Gets up while I'm like fuck'n
BAM! wit my fist, BAM! "Get
Up, nigga! Get up! Ain't got

Time for dis shit." 'N she's like
Bent over between the curb
'N the car, 'n BAM! 'n she

All fat 'n shit, and shakin'
'N I say, "Lissen up, you
Muthafuck'n fat shit, you

Get your BAM! fat ass offa
My street, nigga! Dis my street,
Far as you fuck'n concerned."

'N you fuck'n know what? Next
Time I see her, she all nice
'N shit, 'n I say, "No girl,

You fucked in da head nigga,"
'Cuz I ain't wit dat shit, no fuck
'N way. 'N she's like "Didn't

I see you at Anthony's
Party?" 'N she's all fuck'n
Smilin' 'n shit, 'n I think

What da fuck makes niggas
Put on wit udda niggas?
I'm like "Shit, muthafucka,

Do I know you? Excuse me?"
Shit. D'you fuck'n ever see
Her ass? Dat's her. Da fuck'n

Nigga's always "Charlesgate dis"
'N representin' 'n shit
When she don't know fuck'n shit.

Do you fuck'n believe dat?
Niggas comin' up to you
'N sayin' "Haven't I seen

You at so and so?" What the
Fuck do they think I'm fuckin'
'Spose to say? "Yeah, dat's me. So

Fuck'n what." Don't be askin'
Me where I fuck'n been 'n
Shit. 'Cuz I'm like, fuck, "Do I

Know you?" I'm like, "If you ain't
Got fuck'n anything to
Say, don't say fuck'n nothin'."

Far from Earth

after Sappho

The right-hand ladder rail
    rests on the last round knot
    of a branch as narrow
as the sweat-black handle
    of an ax, or a hoe,
    and when she reaches out
after the ripe apple
    she had missed, or forgot,
    the nervous leaves applaud,
    the barrow far below
tips, or seems to, the pail
hooked to her belt looks full,
    the earth with its shallow
furrows formidable,
    warm, round, sure of her doubt
    and itself. An airplane's shadow
    passes. Then she lets go
of the left ladder rail
    and leans out till she's caught
    her breath and her elbow,
crooked, and the last apple
    blushes in the shadow
of her palm, a cradle
    for apple, first love, taut
breast with no nipple, small
    drum she balances, now
    and then switching hands, now

pressing it to a pale
              cheek, suppressing just how
      hard the rungs underfoot
feel, how much the world swells
under her gradual
              backing down, toward us, how
              good it is to be so
far from earth, smart, careful,
so free from the central
      pull, the low point—how
even this, her apple,
              will be, in that barrow,
      one round, hard, sweet fruit—
indistinguishable.

Passion Fruit

Orange

You—thick-skinned,
Global prison—
What have you pent
Up but ordinary sun,

The spit of Earth's black bread and
Clear rainwater
In your dead-end
Cells? And what inquisitor

Sentenced them—these
Trickles of innocence I set free,
Your navel pressed deep
Into my palm as I squeeze?

Amnesty: drink up.
The acid will arouse
You. An empty house
Makes a good cup.

Grapes

Raindrops accidentally
Double you. These smaller twins
Have no stems

But, upon reflection, cling like family,
Sparkling emblems
Of venial sins.

The same sun under which
You swelled and ripened
Kisses your wet sisters.

One by one, that bitch
Takes her stipend
And leaves blisters.

Apple

Halving you, my thumb
Blushes, the blade
Stops just short of blood,
And the bowl I've made
Holding you brims over.

Gently lifting one face
Loose of its lover
Makes a little moonrise
Over water, an evening
I can be inside.

Your warmth is the warmth
Of my pocket. Your bruises
Map the times I banged
My thighs against hard places.
They are seas.

Like Crises.
Like Tranquility.

Lemon (1)

Every first time I have you in my mouth
I shudder in a place much further south.

Raisins

Pills in bottles.
Bullets in clips.
Little crumbs spittle
Glues to my lips.

Spit wads, syrupy
Changepurses
With scrotal folds each
Kiss rehearses.

One by one or by
Black handfuls, cuds
I suck and I chew and I
Swallow like words—

So careful, careful
Not to overdose
On sweet rocks that rattle
In my vacuum's throat.

Peach

Mattressed by grass, on skinny slats of earth,
I lie long looking up into your skirt—

All whirled bones and stays, dark, knotty hips
And trunk that blot the sun like an eclipse.

A breeze. The fixed stars blink, the planets blush—
Their ripeness, plain as rust, betrays a crush

On me, head cradled in your roots' lap—
Solar, and solo, until your slim stems snap.

Banana (1)

One man's meat:
Singular and vulnerable, contrite,
Stripped bare.

With you bowed like this,
Peel bunched at your feet
Like yellowed underwear,

I have no appetite,
Not even for a kiss.
But oh, when you are supine in a bowl—

When the arc of your back flattens,
Wet with sun—
When your skin blackens,

My mouth makes a hole
For poison.

Watermelon

No matter how it begins, it ends like this:
Black lacquer lozenges spit in concentric rings,
Pale rinds in small pyres, like toenail clippings,
Tap water on my mouth and chin, a piss.

The steps that should bring me back to bed go first
Into the dark kitchen. I turn on a light,
Search cabinets for food, return unsatisfied.
What had seemed like hunger was really thirst.

Index and middle fingers at my lips,
I still smell you, still feel your cool skin
Against my cheek and shoulder in the store,
Vessel of sweet liquor, heavy as sin,
Hard curves whitening my fingertips.
Nothing is left of you. Nothing is more.

Cherries

Bending to pick up laundry
    Still wet with rain, you say:

"The wind *strips* me—"
    But you let them go:

Love's letters,
    These scattered sheaths,

These pale sheets, these
    Fingertips, these scarves,

Swirled ears the wind
    Blows into curves,

Cool lips O-ing so
    The pink, inner blossom shows.

The truth is as you bend
    To pick up laundry

Still wet with rain,
    The wind strips *me.*

Strawberry

As I take my first bite,
Try to concentrate.
Bleed on my incisors,
Let your seeds pock white
Enamel, make me salivate.

Earth-child, let the memory of my lips
Haunt my tongue's rough sex.
You grew ripe on the ground—
The red cradle of my fingertips
Is your apex.

Lemon (2)

Tongue number,
Mouthful of ice, bite
From a box of pins,
My knife makes you smile,
Your smile makes me wince.

Scratch ticket,
Gold coins, bright skin
Under my fingernail—
I spend you in hot tea—
The only lover I inhale.

Banana (2)

From our one nightstand,
In a cone of yellow light,
Your ripening reprimands
Me, night after night.

I might try to touch your
Sugar spots in the dark,
Or try to find your fire
With my spark.

Then we'll spoon like lovers—
Or stubbed out cigarettes—
Smoke circling above us
Like regrets.

Blueberries

Eye-blue,
Staring from the bowl—
Blind pupils,
Hard nipples
In cream cold
As dew.

Ball bearings,
Ink clots
Dark as full stops,
Same steel as my spoon,
I can hold my tongue
Or hold you.

Ellipses,
My lips see you
Better than I do;
Blue pebbles, syllables
I speak more clearly
With my mouth full.

Mango

Green silk, and red silk, and even more
Orange silk where a band of scars
Sings to the knife: "Don't hesitate.
Cut me. It's what you're for,"

And then the newly-wet handle as I slit the rind,
The gentle tugs that expose the flesh,
The letting light in that feels so much
Like opening a blind—

And then the tongue-pit, how stonily it confronts
Its naked reflection in a flowered dish,
While juice pools beneath it like a pouting lip
And I remember how I loved you once.

Notes

The authors of the titles that make up "The Crucible" are MacIntyre, Nolan, Benedict, Hemingway, The Boston Women's Health Care Collective, Agee and Evans, Calvino, Austen, Steiner, Appelfeld, Fitzgerald, Derrida, Richards, Bly, Milton, Jones, Steinberg, Cortazar, Mill, Culler, Freud, Milosz, Paton, Auerbach, Steinbeck, Hemingway, Updike, Lawrence, Dostoevsky, Harris, Sontag, Nabokov, Browning, Borges, (anthology), Freud, Goodman, Angelou, Hemingway, Brodsky, Wolfe, Foucault.

"Pride's Round" is rhetorically based on George Herbert's "Sin's Round."

Poet Christopher Smart suffered from mental illness and was frequently institutionalized.

"The New Life" takes its first line from a poem by Emily Dickinson.

Dr. Johnson (b. 1709) was a poet and lexicographer. Bishop Berkeley (b. 1685) was an Idealist. Telegraph Avenue is the main drag in Berkeley, California.

"Falsetto" is a translation of Eugenio Montale's early poem.

"Ice and Fire" borrows the words that end its lines from Robert Frost's "Fire and Ice."

"Nocturnal Transmission with Imagery as Attachment" remembers Philip

Larkin's "Love Again" (1979).

Derek Walcott is alive and well. The "Pitons" are two peaks near Soufriere, St. Lucia.

"Home Thoughts from Aboard Continental Flight 94" refers to Browning's "Home Thoughts from Abroad"—a theme Joseph Brodsky was quite familiar with. He died in 1996. Much of this poem was drafted en route from Los Angeles to Newark.

"Invitation to Ms. Jorie Graham" is rhetorically based upon Elizabeth Bishop's "Invitation to Miss Marianne Moore."

"Contents of a Jar" is a cento of lines from Wallace Stevens.

The four Tom Hanks poems are rhetorically based on poems by Osip Mandelstam. "'Forrest Gump'…," in particular, is based on "Lines About the Unknown Soldier" composed in Voronezh in 1939.

"BAM!" was overheard on an outbound MBTA Orange Line train.

"Far From Earth" takes a fragment from Sappho as its starting point.